MID-EAST ACES

——The Israeli Air Force Today——

MID-EAST ACES

The Israeli Air Force Today

Philip Handleman

OSPREY
AEROSPACE

In memory to those of the Israeli Air Force who have given their lives. May those who follow know not the sword but the ploughshare.

Published in 1991 by Osprey Publishing Limited
59 Grosvenor Street, London WX 9DA

British Library Cataloguing in Publication Data

Handleman, Philip
   1. Mid-east aces. Air forces.
   I. Israeli air force
   907.8776
ISBN 0 85045 978 8

Editor Dennis Baldry
Page design David Tarbutt
Printed in Hong Kong

Front cover The McDonnell Douglas F-15 Eagle air superiority fighter is the IAF's most formidable deterrent against hostile penetration of Israeli airspace

Title page The aerobatic demonstration team of the IAF operates the Fouga (later Potez/Áerospatiale) Magister, a French jet trainer made famous in the same role by the Patrouille de France and the Belgian Diables Rouges

Back cover A Python 3 infrared-guided dogfight missile poised on the wing pylon of an F-15

Right Israel's major military flight training facility is Hazerim Air Force Base near Beersheba. Here, recently graduated high school students as young as 18 years of age are matriculated into a rigorous two year training programme. The selection process is incredibly stiff, followed by what is surely one of the highest washout rates for any air force in the world

For a catalogue of all books published by Osprey Aerospace
please write to:

**The Marketing Department,
Octopus Illustrated Books, 1st Floor, Michelin House,
81 Fulham Road, London SW3 6RB**

Acknowledgements

The Israel Air Force maintains extremely tight security. Given the IAF's state of constant readiness this is fully understandable, but for the writer/photographer trying to produce a picture book of the modern IAF it makes the task difficult. Without the help of certain dedicated individuals this project would not have come to fruition.

For their assistance, without which this book would not be a reality, I wish to thank Major Orly Gal, Major Giora Kaplan, retired Brigadier General Yacov Terner, Maya Ackerstein of the IAF Museum staff, Captain Jacob Merla, Lieutenant Sharon Shahaf, Lieutenant Nirit Farber, Lieutenant Colonel Irit Atsmon, retired Major Aharon Lapidot of the ISRAEL AIR FORCE MAGAZINE staff, Sergeant Guy Rimon also of the ISRAEL AIR FORCE MAGAZINE staff, and Major General Avihu Ben-Nun.

Special thanks are due to IAF pilots who answered my sometimes naive questions and who provided insight into the workings of the IAF. Security requirements dictate that I refer to them only as Captain A and Major M.

A small number of particularly stunning pictures in this book were provided by the IAF. I am impressed by the superb job done by the IAF's photographers and am grateful to the IAF for its willingness to allow the inclusion of some of its pictures.

Finally, the patience of Mary Heilbronn during my long absences on fact finding and photographic trips is above and beyond the call of duty.

This book, while providing a 'window' into the modern Israeli Air Force is by no means a comprehensive volume. The reader interested in more information may check his public library for the reference works AN ILLUSTRATED GUIDE TO THE ISRAELI AIR FORCE by Bill Gunston (1982) and THE FIGHTING ISRAELI AIR FORCE by Stanley M Ulanoff and David Eshel (1985). Also, the IAF published a history (primarily in Hebrew) entitled OPEN SKIES edited by Aharon Lapidot (1988). Additionally, the publications ISRAEL AIR FORCE MAGAZINE (primarily in Hebrew) and IDF JOURNAL are published in Israel and are available on a subscription basis.

בסיס חיל־האויר חצרים
ברוכים הבאים
WELCOME
HAZERIM AIR FORCE BASE

Introduction

The Israel Air Force counts among its missions air superiority, close air support, airlift and special operations. From its austere beginnings with the modern State of Israel's creation in 1948, the IAF has performed its missions remarkably well. Almost always massively outgunned in its major wars of the past forty some years, the IAF has always managed to score decisive victories—leading to a deserved mystique.

Ruling the region's airspace is crucial to maintaining the advantage in any major Mid-east conflict. Israel is keenly aware that without control of the skies its prospects in an all out land battle would be dismal at best. Accordingly, the IAF puts a premium on its air-to-air fighting component. The IAF throughout its history has demonstrated its dogfighting prowess, most notably with the lopsided results from the 1982 confrontation with Syrian MiGs over the Bekaa Valley.

Providing cover for ground forces is another prerequisite for victory in high intensity Mid-east warfare. More than once the tank columns and infantry brigades of the Israeli Defence Forces have broken out of an otherwise untenable position because of the timely and effective intervention of IAF airpower. Since all military flying in Israel is the responsibility of the IAF, even the helicopter gunships such as the Bell AH-1 Cobra belong to the IAF and are flown by IAF pilots. This minimizes service rivalry. In fact, the IAF pilots consider their branch of the military to be an integral part of the IDF. It is common for IAF pilots to talk of themselves as members of the Israeli Army. As a self-contained fighting unit, the IDF is analogous to the US Marine Corps. This is a particular benefit in the pursuit of the air/land battle for there tends to be much better coordination between ground and air forces than if each branch of service were genuinely autonomous.

Getting men and supplies to the battle in time is vital for Israel is a small country whose fragile geography could be quickly violated. Roads to the nation's extremities and the countryside's rugged terrain make transportation by air a virtual necessity, especially when the IDF is on short notice.

IAF pilots seem justifiably obsessed with the notion that their nation's very survival hinges on the job they do. This view necessitates that each IAF pilot excel. The IAF pilot flies his airplane in every battle as though it is not only his life at stake but the lives and liberty of all his countrymen that are at stake. He, like all members of the IDF, has pledged that never again will Israelis face the tragic end that befell their ancestors who from the fortress atop Masada courageously fought back the Romans until overpowered by vastly superior numbers in 73 AD.

The modern Israeli Air Force in circumstance and character is notably reminiscent of the Royal Air Force of 1940 which during the Battle of Britain repulsed a seemingly unstoppable enemy and in doing so altered the course of history. Evident at every level of today's IAF is an *esprit de corps* that conveys a sense of being able to accomplish any task. This pride, instilled largely during the tenure of IAF Commander Ezer Weizman (himself a former RAF fighter pilot), is an important ingredient that holds the IAF in good stead as it faces such new threats as state-of-the-art Soviet fighters in the air forces of Syria and Iraq and the growing surface-to-surface missile menace. Major General Avihu Ben-Nun, the IAF's current Commander and an accomplished fighter pilot, carries on the IAF's impressive leadership tradition, contributing to this air force's mystique.

Right An otherwise non-descript wall near a covered parking ramp at Hazerim Air Force Base sports a colourful profile portrait of the Fouga Magister, the IAF's longtime primary jet trainer

Contents

Air defence and attack

Left Among the most serious threats to Israel in today's high technology warfare environment is the presence of chemical agents with an apparently growing delivery capability among nations in the region. Here IAF pilots are shown in front of their F-15 Eagle fighter attired in special suits to protect against poisonous gases. Training in such apparel, though accentuating the already high ambient temperatures, is a regular occurrence at IAF bases. The IAF hopes that its dominance of the skies will serve to deter its potential adversaries from using chemical agents in battle with Israel

Below The IAF has consistently maintained an enviable level of *esprit de corps*. IAF pilots and ground crews take immense pride in their units. Like so many great air forces in history, the IAF permits squadrons to adopt distinct emblems and badges. While the IAF's tight security generally does not allow a unit emblem to be associated in public with a particular squadron, occasionally some of the unique markings of the IAF are publicly unveiled. This cartoon-like bird's head decorates the vertical tail of an IAF F-15

Below A Boeing 707 reconfigured for refuelling missions is shown in a mock refuelling flight with A-4 Skyhawks 'feeding' off the wingtip hoses and an F-15 trailing behind the tail boom

Right An F-15 soars straight up in an impressive performance of the sleek air superiority fighter's performance

Left With afterburners lit, the McDonnell Douglas F-15 Eagle's two powerful Pratt & Whitney F100 turbofan engines push the fighter farther and faster into the accommodating crystal clear Mid-east sky

Below Perhaps no other modern fighter aircraft has caught the fancy of the Israeli public as much as the F-15. As the aircraft generally considered to be the West's leading air superiority fighter, the Eagle is perceived as essential to the preservation of secure Israeli airspace. Air superiority is widely recognized as a prerequisite to the maintenance of Israeli security and to victory in any major Mid-east conflict

The graceful lines of the Eagle are apparent in this profile view. F-15s were first delivered to Israel in 1976

Four victory marks are painted on the nose of this F-15, nicknamed 'Star' in Hebrew. The F-15 has proved to be an effective fighter in skirmishes with hostile forces, particularly against the Syrians over the Bekaa Valley in June 1982. The IAF paved the way for what has come to be known as the Bekaa Valley turkey shoot by destroying 17 of the 19 Syrian surface-to-air missile (SAM) batteries. With the Syrian air defences so weakened, the IAF fighters were able to dominate, resulting in the lopsided score of about 80 kills to no losses. Demonstrating its mission versatility, the F-15 also participated in the bombing attack on the Palestine Liberation Organization headquarters in Tunis

Preceding page This F-15 strikes a formidable pose while on display at Hazerim Air Force base. The presence of F-15s in the IAF inventory has successfully deterred Syria from using its MiG-25s to fly reconnaissance missions over Israel

Above The Israelis developed their own air-to-air heat-seeking missile based on the well regarded American Sidewinder. The Shafir, as the Israeli heat-seeker came to be known, has since been updated and improved. Called the Python 3, this AAM has canard controls and freely pivoting rollerons. Note the yellow cover with handle, obscuring the nose-mounted optical telescope used to focus the heat of the target aircraft on the missile's infrared sensor

A larger and more costly AAM is the radar-guided Sparrow. These fuselage-mounted missiles are marked 'Airborne Inert', indicating that they are used for training purposes

Left MiG-killer: the six victory symbols on the nose of this F-15 Eagle are the result of combats with Syrian MiG-21 and MiG-23 fighters over the Bekaa Valley in 1982. Although it's conceivable that all six victories were the work of one pilot, the kills probably belong to the aircraft. This F-15 is carrying its full war fit of four Python 3 infrared-guided AAMs, four AIM-7 Sparrow semi-active radar-guided AAMs, and a centreline combat-rated external fuel tank. In common with other front-line air assets in the IAF, the F-15 is fitted with Israeli electronic warfare systems, including radar warning receivers (RWR) and identification friend or foe (IFF). During the Gulf War in 1991, Israeli F-15 pilots maintained round-the-clock cockpit readiness to guard against Iraqi air attacks

Below Vital air superiority would not be accomplished in the treacherous Mideast skies were it not for superb airborne surveillance and communications made possible by aircraft like the Grumman E-2C Hawkeye. The E-2C, with its radar rotodome perched atop its fuselage, serves as part of 'the eyes and ears' of the Israeli Defence Forces

An aircraft developed to provide the US Navy with an expanded fleet air defence perimeter, the Hawkeye has been used by the IAF to detect hostile Arab fighters and direct IAF defenders to intercept them. Originally designed as a carrier-based aircraft, the short take-off and landing capability of the Hawkeye is an added benefit enjoyed by the IAF

Below This General Dynamics F-16 (its tail section shown here) was publicly displayed at Hazerim Air Force Base. While the IAF has traditionally guarded its squadron markings, the F-16's fin artwork with a staggered lighting bolt is suggestive of a biblical theme. The elongated pod between the engine nozzle section and the fin houses electronic countermeasures equipment

Left While the F-16 Fighting Falcon has been effective in its intended purpose of close-in dogfighting, it was used with outstanding results in the 7 June 1981 bombing mission against the Osirak nuclear reactor in Iraq. With surgical precision, eight F-16s unloaded their bombs, destroying the nuclear reactor then under construction, the bi-products from which were reportedly going to be used to manufacture nuclear weapons to be deployed against Israel

Despite the introduction of the Python 3, the IAF still has substantial stocks of the classic Sidewinder AAM, two drill rounds of which are seen mounted on this F-16C. The IAF is expected to receive the fire-and-forget Advanced Medium Range Air-to-Air Missile (AMRAAM) for its F-15s and F-16s

The IAF has a fleet of more than 150 Fighting Falcons, the majority being
F-16C/D models. A high proportion of Israeli avionics were incorporated into
the 75 F-16C/Ds supplied by the US government under the Peace Marble III
programme announced in April 1988

Above An IAF F-16D in appropriate camouflage paint scheme roars off into the desert sky

Right As this two-seat F-16D combat-capable trainer rolls, the overhead planform view becomes apparent. Diminutive IAF insignia (a blue Star of David in a solid white circle—the colours of the Israeli flag) are emblazoned on the wings. Wingtip-mounted AAMs are characteristic of the F-16; either Sidewinders (as here), or Python 3s

Close air support is a critical part of the IAF mission. An F-16 swoops down to release its bomb load for some target practice against the hollow shells of old trucks in an awesome demonstration of destructive capability. Flares are dispensed to ward off incoming heat-seeking missiles

Above A bad guy's eye view of an F-16C Fighting Falcon: note the prominent panoramic canopy, large ventral jet intake, deployed leading edge slats and airbrakes, wingtip Sidewinders and streamlined centreline fuel tank

Right Roll 'em: caught in the break, this F-16 reveals a large bomb dispenser underwing and the rectangular chaff/flare ejection ports between the wing trailing edge and horizontal stabilizer

Left Today the financially strapped IAF still utilizes the Skyhawk in the ground attack role, but the aircraft is also employed to introduce trainee fighter pilots to the fast-jet environment. Elongated tailcones were retrofitted to IAF A-4s mostly to minimize the risk of engine damage in the event of the aircraft being struck in the rear by a heat-seeking missile—especially the man-portable Soviet SA-7 *Grail.* As the A-4 is powered by a single Pratt & Whitney J52 turbojet, this Israeli innovation has undoubtedly prevented many IAF pilots from becoming POWs (or worse)

Below This A-4s tail art reveals the haunting image of a large-jawed creature with wings. The symbology painted on IAF aircraft is almost always small, thereby carefully ensuring no significant interruption of the camouflage scheme

A sampling of the mighty ordnance load the A-4N can carry—but not all at once! IAF Skyhawks are fitted with two French DEFA 553 cannons of 30 mm calibre—unlike all US versions which have 20 mm Mk 12 cannons as standard

Once the IAF's principal air superiority fighter, the F-4E Phantom II currently equips five attack squadrons; the still highly secret RF-4E reconnaissance version is operated by one special unit

Preceding pages The Phantom 2000, shown here is an attractive multi-coloured camouflage paint scheme, is a vastly improved version of the venerable F-4E. The Israeli Air Force and the Israeli aerospace industry are famous for eking out extra performance from current and older production aircraft through modifications designed to suit the needs of Mid-east air warfare. Retaining General Electric J79 turbojets, but incorporating a totally new nav/attack system, the Phantom 2000 is said to be as formidable in the strike role as any aircraft rolling off the production lines today. The Phantom 2000 achieved operational status with the IAF in 1989

Left Another angle of the Phantom 2000 provides a fresh view of this handsome aircraft and a reminder of the lineage of the widely used McDonnell Douglas F-4 airframe—from the air battles of Vietnam to the contested skies over the Sinai

Above A close-up of the Phantom 2000's tail section provides a rare opportunity to see IAF markings

For visitors to Hazerim Air Force Base, a mannequin is dressed in the flight outfit of the Phantom 2000 pilot. The boiling temperatures of the midday Negev would make this pose exceedingly uncomfortable for a real pilot after a minute or two

Now a museum piece, the Dassault-Brequet Mirage IIIC represents the culmination of the IAF's 'French Period'. Ordered in 1959, before the tailless delta-winged technology of the French fighter was proven, the Mirage, delivered in 1962, provided the IAF with its first Mach 2 capability. In IAF hands the Mirage became the first aircraft to shoot down a MiG-21. Later in the lightning raids against Arab air forces during the first few hours of the Six Day War in June 1967, the Mirage expanded on its reputation as a superb fighter, accumulating a superb kill ratio. The stunning success of the IAF in the Six Day War elevated the status of both the IAF and the French aviation industry. However, in June 1967 the French government manifested a change in foreign policy by embargoing arms shipments, including Mirage spares, to Israel

Above Flown by a number of different pilots, this Mirage has shot down 13 Arab aircraft during its career with the IAF. The IAF probably has more jet aces than any other airforce in the world

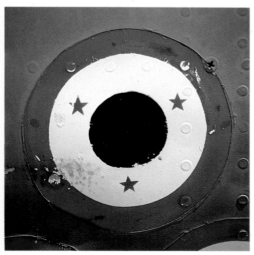

Left The IAF scrupulously guards the identity of its aces and indeed of all its pilots. The threat of terrorist reprisal mandates this strict security

The trademark features of the Mirage—a delta configuration with an absence of horizontal tail surfaces—can be easily appreciated from this angle

With a shaky foreign supply line for much of its defence needs, as evidenced by the critically timed French embargo, Israel sought to at least partially offset its reliance on overseas sources by developing a near full scale 'in house' design and production capability. The first fruit borne of this effort was the Nesher, an enhanced version of the Mirage. An even more improved type was the Kfir C.2, followed by the digitally controlled and aerodynamically refined Kfir C.7. The Kfir, pictured here in both low visibility grey and standard tan and green tactical camouflage, is a Mach 2-class fighter. The installation of the more powerful and economical General Electric J79 turbojet in place of the French SNECMA Atar powerplant gives the Kfir rapid acceleration and an outstanding engage/disengage capability. Indeed, the US Navy and Marines have used the Kfir under lease in dissimilar air combat manoeuvring training as its speed simulates the potential of certain Soviet fighters. Today's fighters, however, can sustain high rates of turn, and the Kfir is somewhat limited in this respect; its primary purpose in the modern IAF is now ground attack. The Kfir requires long stretches of runway for take-off and landing, which many battlefield planners would consider a distinct disadvantage owing to the notion that a sophisticated enemy would attempt to crater his opponent's runways, rendering such runways useless for all but the true V/STOL (vertical/short take-off and landing) aircraft. The IAF does not appear particularly concerned with this problem since the primary IAF mission remains air superiority. As long as the IAF succeeds in this mission, so the theory goes, its bases should be protected

Transports and tank-killers

Left A workhorse for many air forces around the world, the legendary Lockheed C-130 Hercules here performs a JATO (jet assisted take-off). The heat generated from the blast is quite intense, but extra thrust is provided for lifting heavy loads out of short airstrips

Below The C-130 is used to haul troops and cargo to the battlefield. This sturdy four-engined turboprop, with its large load carrying capability and short field characteristics, has saved the day on the Mid-east battlefield by airlifting reinforcements and supplies to the centre of the action just when needed. Perhaps the Herk's greatest feat was its use in Operation Thunderbolt, the historic July, 1976 rescue of passengers of an Air France airliner hijacked by terrorists and diverted to Uganda's Entebbe International Airport. IAF C-130s, in a brilliantly planned and executed mission, landed at Entebbe and spirited the hostages to Israel on, as fate would have it, the bicentennial of American independence

Above The IAF operates around 20 C-130s, including at least two KC-130H flight refuelling tankers. Sporting an interesting unit marking on the tail, this 'Fat Albert' delivers its cargo using the low-altitude parachute extraction system (LAPES) method

Right A major component of the IAF's heavy lift capability rests on the broad shoulders of the Sikorsky CH-53. Approaching at a fast clip with landing gear retracted, the massive helicopter's rotor blades churn the early evening air

Above From this perspective, the CH-53's long flight refuelling probe can be seen jutting out from the pudgy nose of the heavy chopper

Right The IAF's CH-53 fleet is currently being modernized, Project Yasour 2000 being designed to extend their service lives and improve reliability. The CH-53 has a crew of three and can accommodate up to 55 troops, or 24 stretcher cases, or other internal loads such as a $1\frac{1}{2}$ ton truck, or external underslung loads such as a 105 mm howitzer

A CH-53 passes over some of the rugged Mid-east terrain. The helicopter's tactical paint scheme blends with the sandy tone of the parched mountains below. The IAF operates the CH-53D, a version originally introduced into service by the US Marine Corps

Shortly after the CH-53's delivery to the IAF in 1969, two of the behemoths were used to scoop out a then sophisticated Soviet radar system from Egyptian territory and return it to Israel. Such legendary exploits are the basis for the mystique associated with Israeli Air Force

In a patriotic display during the opening of the IAF flight school's Graduation Day ceremony, Bell 205 'Hueys' pass in review towing Israeli flags. Rotary-wing aircraft in the IAF, as with many military forces throughout the world, have taken on increased importance

Left This is the Bell 212, a derivative of the Bell 205. The main difference is that the 212, which entered IAF service about eight years following the 205's introduction to the IAF in the late 1960s, has two engines. The 212's Pratt & Whitney PT6 Twin Pac coupled turboshafts enable this tractable machine to operate with greater lifting efficiency in high temperatures

Right Sitting passively on the ramp is a Bell 206 JetRanger. This hugely successful helicopter is used by the IAF for VIP transport, patrol missions and communications

Above A Bell JetRanger shares parking space with a Beechcraft Queen Air. The twin Beech is used for C-130 pilot conversion training, VIP transport and priority deliveries

Right During the non-stop aerial display of Graduation Day, a Bell 206, known in the US military as the OH-58 Kiowa or Scout, banks tightly and activates a skid-mounted smoke system. The red plume and nose light add colour to the desert sky

Above left Peering below, one of the chopper pilots scans the landscape. Some years ago it was considered a form of put-down for cadets at the IAF flight school to obtain a helicopter training assignment. That attitude has thankfully been reversed. Now helicopters are considered as vital to the front-line combat effort as their fixed-winged counterparts. IAF helicopter pilots need no longer suffer an inferiority complex

Below left This JetRanger demonstrates that because temperatures reach such high levels in the desert, IAF helicopters usually fly with doors removed

Right As part of the Graduation Day ceremony, Five Bell JetRangers formate to perform a series of impressive precision manoeuvres. Four outer team members are swinging around the team leader, who remains in the centre hovering stationary

Above The Israelis harbour a genuine fondness for the Piper Cub. In the difficult early days of the modern State of Israel, when the government was just trying to assemble an air force, the little puddle jumper from William Piper's factory in Lock Haven, Pennsylvania was actually used on bombing missions. From its beginnings in the late 1940s, the IAF built its justly deserved reputation for innovation. The Cub has made such an indelible impression on the Israeli public that commonly the average Israeli refers to any light aircraft as 'those Pipers'. Today the Piper Super Cub is used by the flight school at Hazerim Air Force Base for the first several hours of cadet flight time—not so much for training as for screening purposes. The Super Cub is painted in standard IAF training colours

Right The odd looking but very capable Dornier Do 28 Skyservant serves as a light transport capable of short field operations. It is one of the few tailwheel aircraft in the IAF and provides a bit of a challenge to the pilot when landing in a brisk crosswind

The McDonnell Douglas (formerly Hughes) 500MD TOW Defender is armed with four tube-launched optically tracked wire-guided anti-armour missiles

This close-up view of the 500MD TOW Defender highlights the nose-
mounted sight (the blunt edge emanating from the left side of the nose) as well
as the side-mounted missile racks

Left A Defender flies very low to the ground where it would ordinarily be flown in combat as a means to avoid enemy detection. The agile Defender with its TOW missile system has been effective in the anti-tank role for the IAF

Above The Bell AH-1 Cobra is an awesome close air support aircraft, seen here over a column of tanks of the Israeli Defence Forces. The Cobra possesses devastating firepower in the form of its 20 mm chin cannon, TOW missiles and 2.75 inch rockets. Like the Defender, the Cobra has successfully performed its tank-buster mission. Cobras have been in IAF hands since shortly after the Yom Kippur War

Left Combat proven during the Vietnam War, where it accumulated more than one million flight hours between June 1967 and March 1973, the Cobra continues to set the standard by which other anti-tank helicopters are judged. The AH-1S version operated by the IAF is equipped with a laser rangefinder, an engine heat suppressor to minimize infrared signature, an infrared jammer and a radar warning receiver (RWR) linked with an AN/ALQ-136 jamming system

Right The Dauphin 2 incorporates a number of important innovations pioneered by the helicopter division of Aérospatiale, one of the most impressive being the all-plastic Starflex rotor head

Left A 1984 addition to the Israeli inventory was the Aérospatiale SA.365 Dauphin 2 shown here low over the Mediterranean. In Israel, all military flying is done by the IAF so even ship-borne helicopters of the Israeli Navy, like some of the Dauphins, are operated by IAF pilots. Note the large rescue hoist protruding from the chopper's fuselage

Above A Dauphin 2 cruises over the historic Old City of Jerusalem. The orange and white colours are something of an anomaly for IAF aircraft—in the case of the Dauphin they point out its special mission as a rescue helicopter. The Dauphin 2 is certainly no slouch, being capable of speeds up to 190 mph

IAF Museum

Below Displayed under the blazing desert sun is a vintage Mikoyan MiG-21 *Fishbed* fighter. Israel is a land steeped in history and not surprisingly the IAF believes it is important to preserve not only its own aircraft but those of its past belligerents

Overleaf The camouflaged fuselage of this MiG-21 cuts an attractive image against the blue of the Negev sky. The aircraft's belly is white, presumably for blending into a less hospitable sky. An Israeli Star of David adorns the MiG's fuselage

Developed from the classic MiG-15, which it superseded in production in 1953, the MiG-17 *Fresco* was a significant tactical airpower asset for the Egyptian and Syrian air forces until the mid-1970s. Armament comprised three 23 mm NR-23 cannons, four rocket pods or two 250 kg bombs

As many American pilots had discovered to their cost in Vietnam, the MiG-17 was a tough, highly manoeuvrable fighter. The *Fresco C* version flown by the North Vietnamese was also delivered to many Arab air forces, its afterburning Klimov VK-1A turbojet endowing the aircraft with a spritely performance

Among the earliest jet-powered adversaries the IAF faced was the MiG-15 *Fagot*. As a fighter, the MiG-15 outclassed the Gloster Meteors and Dassault Ouragans delivered to the IAF, but the introduction of the Dassault Mystère IVA in the mid-1950s allowed the Israelis to establish a measure of technical superiority over its Arab opponents

Tucked in a corner of Hazerim Air Force Base is the impressive but little
known Israeli Air Force Museum. The Museum, which boasts a total of 80
aircraft in its collection (about 15 of the mainly older ones are flyable), has been
off limits to the general public. The IAF, always mindful of security, has been
reluctant to allow the public to set foot on an IAF installation. Accordingly,
only IAF personnel and invited guests have been granted access. This may
change if a plan for open admission is put into effect. A prize of the Museum
collection is this Dassault Super Mystère fighter bomber—a sleek French
design which first flew on 2 March 1955. Similar in appearance to the North
American F-100 Super Sabre, from which the Dassault design derived its
flattened nose and 45-degree wing sweep, the Super Mystère could easily
exceed Mach 1 in level flight.

Above As was the case in the British Royal Air Force, in Israeli parlance the Douglas DC-3/C-47 is the Dakota. Like such legendary aeroplanes as the Cub and the Spitfire, this classic among classics has captured the affection of generations of Israelis. Its unstinting service in an amazing variety of transport roles over many years has endeared this wonderful aircraft to the citizenry it has served. As a tribute to its longevity, the IAF acquired additional DC-3s in the mid-1970s to replace the jaded Nord Noratlases which were purchased twenty years earlier, ironically, to replace the DC-3s! In fact, the sheer reliability of the 'Dak' can be admired not only through the memories associated with this museum piece, but by the deep hum of the Pratt & Whitney radial engines which continue to lumber the aircraft through Israeli airspace

Right Reflective of the IAF's 'French Period' are these three Sud Aviation Vautours. Most of the IAF's Vautours were of the bomber type and made their greatest contribution in the Six Day War during attacks on airbases in Iraq and Egypt. Arab forces were threatening Israel, and rather than waiting for the first blow to be delivered the IAF staged devastating pre-emptive raids which in a few hours decimated the air forces of the opposing powers. The bomb loads of the Vautours were directed with major success at, among other targets, the dreaded Tupolev Tu-16 *Badger* medium bomber which were armed with AS-2 *Kipper* stand-off missiles

This Boeing Stearman has obviously seen better days. A creature of neglect as a result of the IAF Museum's limited resources, this Stearman was one of many converted into crop sprayers. No doubt the prolonged use of chemicals ate into the aircraft's surface. The burdensome sun has also taken its toll on the fabric

The inauspicious beginnings of the IAF date to the time the modern State of Israel was created in the late 1940s, when such light two-seaters as the Cub, Auster and Taylorcraft served as the fledgling Air Force's 'do-everything' aeroplanes. Stories abound of pilots in those early days trying to hold their featherweight steeds steady while a passenger imitating a bombardier tossed out homemade explosives at attacking Arab cavalrymen on camelback. Those not embellishing these stories of primitive air attack admit that while some of the enemy may have been thrown from their mounts, the damage was more psychological than physical. Today some of these aircraft are on display at the IAF Museum near the 'heavy iron' that arrived later as the IAF progressed toward its status as a world class air force

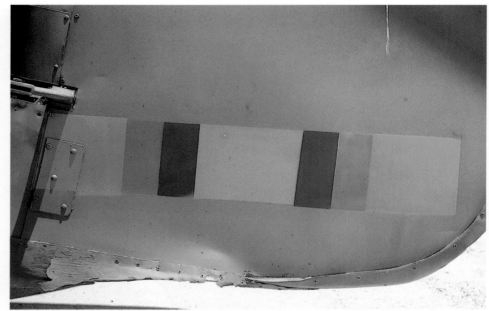

Left One of the most durable aircraft ever built, the North American AT-6 Texan was known to most air forces outside of the United States, including the IAF, as the Harvard—a name given to the aircraft by the British Royal Air Force. This no-nonsense trainer took the cadets through primary or basic flight training, where landings and fundamental aircraft control were mastered, before they progressed to higher speeds and systems complexity. Because the IAF was so pressed for combat aircraft in its formative stages, the Harvard was used in the ground attack role during the War of Independence in 1948

Above Although the IAF is famous (perhaps infamous!) for eschewing pomp and circumstance, the trappings and fanfare of military life, this Harvard has had its rudder decorated with a symbol of its past

The IAF Museum is now home to several Harvards, including this one painted in a combat colour scheme

When the Harvard had outlived its usefulness as a ground attack machine and as the sophistication of the IAF grew through the 1950s, the Harvard was relegated to the training mission exclusively. Thus assigned, The Harvard adopted the standard training colour of all yellow as depicted in this shining restoration

Left In a land rampant with antiquity, no flying antique is as well recognized or imports as much of a sense of the drama of Israel's modern history as the 'black Spitfire'. As Israel struggled for its very survival in the late 1940s, a coterie of IAF pilots provided air defence with Spitfires purchased from Czechoslovakia. Ezer Weizman, a former RAF fighter pilot and nephew of Israel's first president, flew this very Spitfire and insisted on the IAF retaining it after all the others were sold to Burma. Weizman rose to become the IAF Commander and reportedly would give this Spitfire a workout in his free time. Now this valuable beauty is said to be flown occasionally by Danny Shapira, who before retirement was one of Israel's foremost test pilots. The black Spitfire, a Mark 9E, prominently features a rear-view mirror atop the bullet-proof windscreen. Like the majority of Spitfires, the Mark 9 does not have a bubble canopy, so it is imperative that the pilot have a means of checking his six o'clock position

Inset The Israeli Air Force insignia is emblazoned in bright colours on the Spitfire's nose

Above Markings on the Spitfire's elevator are in Hebrew. It is not uncommon in today's IAF for aircraft markings and instrument labels to be written in Hebrew, English and French. While there is no formal requirement that IAF pilots be multilingual, they need to know enough of these languages to properly handle their aircraft. The Spitfire displays the IAF Museum symbol on the fin

The North American P-51 Mustang, considered by some observers to be the best multi-role fighter of World War 2, came into IAF service during the War of Independence. In 1956 during the Sinai Campaign it was the then obsolete piston-engined Mustangs that were used deliberately to sever Egyptian telephone lines with their propellers as they sped low to the ground. The idea was to hamper Egyptian communications shortly before the surprise drop of Israeli paratroopers in the Mitla Pass. This typically outlandish IAF innovation succeeded as usual

The Grumman Avenger carrier-borne torpedo bomber and attack aircraft was known as the TBF except for those manufactured by General Motors which were known as TBMs. This absolutely pristine Avenger restoration is painted in British Fleet Air Arm markings. It is the IAF Museum's mission to obtain and to preserve not only all the aircraft that served with the IAF but also those of occupying and adversarial air forces

Left The Nord Noratlas was an effective transport aircraft, employing a twin-boom design that was particularly well suited to air-dropping heavy loads and paratroops

Above The Boeing Stratocruiser luxury airliner was acquired as surplus by the IAF and used effectively as a heavylift cargo carrier. Some of the voluminous 'Statuscruisers' were used as flight refuelling tankers much as the US Air Force's KC-97 version. A tail marking common to many IAF transports in the Museum shows an eagle's wings bracketing a globe of the Earth which prominently features the Mid-east

Above The Boeing 707, no stranger to El Al (Israel's international commercial air carrier), has served in a variety of roles with the IAF, from electronic warfare to flight refuelling tanker. This example is currently missing its horizontal stabilizers and elevators—parts which may have been cannibalized to keep an IAF 707 operational. Eventually, according to the Museum, this majestic jetliner will be transformed into a theatre for visitors. In the meantime, the aircraft occupies a specially fabricated circular cobblestone parking ramp

Right Helicopters have for a long time played a key role in IAF operations. This Sikorsky S-58, also known as the CH-34, served as a multi-purpose hauler for the IAF during the 1960s

Left Powered by a single 1525 hp Wright R-1820-84 piston-engine, the S-58 was a genuine workhorse, airlifting important supplies to the front as well as transporting up to 18 troops—often to carry out operations behind enemy lines

Above This marking, attached to the S-58's tail, apparently represents a helicopter's swirling rotor blades in the form of swords

The load carrying and short field capabilities of the Swiss Pilatus Turbo Porter made it a welcome addition to the IAF in 1963. Former Israeli Prime Minister Daved Ben Gurion flew as a passenger in this aircraft from his retirement at Kibbutz Sde Boker. The great statesman's wife, Paula, when seeing the Turbo Porter, reportedly dubbed it 'the big Piper'

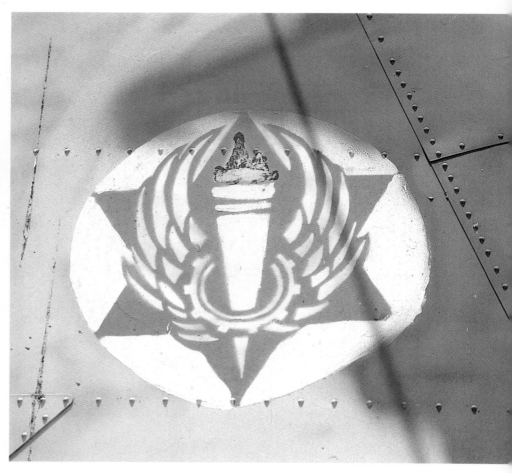

Left The Britten-Norman Islander, by far the most successful product of Britain's post-war light aircraft industry, served in the IAF as a utility and training machine. The disarmed bombs on the Museum ramp are part of a larger display of IAF ordnance and weaponry

Above Among the many markings exhibited at the IAF Museum is this example carried by the Islander—a lit torch amid the Star of David

Above Like many air forces, including its Arab adversaries, the IAF's introduction to the jet age came in the form of the trusty Gloster Meteor, Britain's first jet fighter, the prototype of which first flew on 5 March 1943. The first officially recognized downing of Arab jets in an all jet battle occurred in September 1955 when two Egyptian de Havilland Vampires (ironically also of British origin) penetrated Israeli airspace

Right Another view of the Meteor, this particular example being a tandem-seat NF.13 night fighter designed and built by Armstrong Whitworth. A Syrian Air Force Meteor NF.13 intercepted and destroyed a snooping RAF Canberra PR.7 when it descended to low altitude during a reconnaissance mission launched from Cyprus on 6 November 1956

Tough, simple and highly manoeuvrable, the Ouragan made its maiden flight on 28 February 1949, being the first in a series of outstanding jet fighters created by Marcel Dassault. The Ouragan proved itself during the Six Day War of June 1967, where it wrought havoc in the ground attack role

Soon superceding the intermediate Mystère II in French Air Force service, the
Mystère IVA was, like the earlier Ouragan, also exported to India as well as
Israel. Capable of 615 mph at height thanks to its sharply swept (41-degree)
wing and 3500 kg-thrust Hispano-Suiza Verdon 350 turbojet, the Mystère IVA
had the measure of its opponents during the Sinai Campaign of 1956

The Super Mystère was the IAF's principal air superiority fighter from the late-1950s until Dassault's next generation fighter, the tailless Mirage IIIC, arrived in time for the landmark Six Day War. As in the case of the A-4 Skyhawk, the Super Mystère's elongated tailcone provided worthwhile protection against heat-seeking missiles

Nicknamed 'Big Brother', this particularly interesting exhibit is a reconnaissance version of the French SO.4050 Vautour bomber. The story is told that the Vautour's cameraman in the normal course of operations had to lay flat in the nose of the aircraft. On return to home base after a reconnaissance flight, a Vautour experienced a hydraulic problem causing the landing gear to stick in the retracted position and forcing the pilot into a belly landing. Needless to say, the cameraman's vantage point was terrifying. Though the airmen aboard survived the ordeal without a scratch, the cameraman refused to climb aboard a Vautour for six months

Most of the Vautours supplied to Israel were ex-CFAS (French Strategic Air Command) IIB bomber versions, these entering IAF service in the early 1960s to augment the Vautour IIAs supplied earlier. Interestingly, this Vautour (known as 'Phantomas') is a II.1N night fighter converted to perform electronic warfare duties

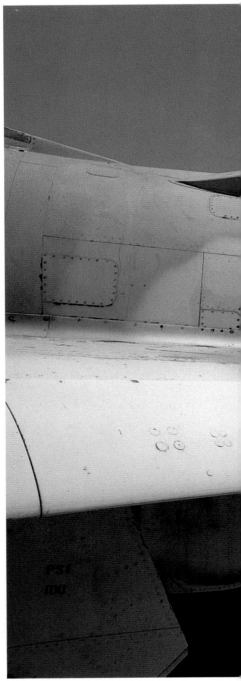

Above Israel responded to the French embargo of the 50 Mirage 5s she had already bought and paid for (as well as helped to develop), by sending agents from Mossad, the secret intelligence service, to obtain the design drawings of the Mirage fighter. Israel Aircraft Industries (IAI), was given the job of manufacturing a near-identical copy of the Mirage which became known as the Nesher. Shown here is the Technolog, a modified Nesher which was used as a development aircraft for the subsequent Kfir programme

Right A closer look at the Technolog, showing the canard as well as the green and two-tone brown camouflage scheme. Another IAI fighter programme, this time of almost totally indigenous design (the major exception being the American Pratt & Whitney PW1120 turbofan), was the Lavi. Unfortunately, after experiencing cost overruns and encountering stiff international opposition, the Lavi programme was cancelled in 1987—despite the fact that two prototypes had already flown and were performing well. However, some of the Lavi's advanced systems and avionics have been incorporated into IAF Kfirs and F-16s

IAF aerobats

In the late 1940s, as a beseiged Israel sought to piece together a viable air force, it obtained a small number of war surplus Boeing Stearman primary trainers from the United States. When this rugged old open cockpit biplane turns gracefully to a point in the empty sky, the sun unwittingly causing the wings to glisten, the radial engine droning in the distance, all men of the air can join in appreciation

Above and left Piloted today by retired IAF Brigadier General Yacov Terner, the silver IAF Museum's silver Stearman thrills audiences at special events throughout the country. General Terner, a former Commander of the IAF flight school at Hazerim Air Force Base and now head of the IAF Museum, delights in zooming down low before airshow crowds. He fastens a red streamer aft of his open cockpit to give the appearance of a long flowing silk scarf. The red streamer is clearly visible as General Terner swoops in for another low pass along the crowd line

The IAF Museum collection already includes a few Fouga Magisters—this example is decorated in the blue and white colours of Israel. Given the age and constant work of the IAF trainers, it is probably not far off when the IAF Museum will take delivery of more of these aircraft

The Fouga Magister has been given a new lease of life by the IAF. The aircraft has been substantially updated with, for example, a new flight control system. The modifications have extended the service life of this primary trainer, now called Tsukit by the IAF. These delightful jet trainers were pressed into service as light attack aircraft during the Six Day War

Left On Graduation Day at the huge training facility, Hazerim Air Force Base, an awkward formation led by a Beechcraft Queen Air flies directly over the reviewing stands. Two Tsukits and two Skyhawks, all used in training, take part in the unusual fly-over

Above A wall at the Hazerim Air Force Base, where the Tsukit is a constant feature in the sky, is decorated with a kind of mural that shows three of the trainers in profile

Left One of the few glimpses the public gets of the vaunted Israeli Air Force is in the form of performances given by the IAF aerobatic demonstration team. Unfortunately, strict IAF security rules prohibit the names and photographs of the faces of current IAF pilots (with the sole exception of the IAF Commander), from being publicly released. Therefore, not even the aerobatic dcemonstration team members are known by name

Above Performing an immaculate loop, the IAF aerobatic demonstration team shows the results of its practice and skill. The team displays at special events throughout the country, serving to entertain large numbers of Israelis and to encourage aspiring pilots

Left The team cascades through a beautiful blue sky with virtually matchless consistency

Above A team aircraft making a lone pass shows the distinctive 'V' or butterfly tail of the old Fouga Magister, the prototype of which first flew on 23 July 1952. Despite modifications leading to a service life extension, the Tsukit, proudly having given many fine pilots their first taste of real flying, will probably have to give way to a new trainer within several years. After about thirty years of valuable IAF service, this petite and noisy trainer of French origin that gave so many cadets their wings (some of whom went on to ace status in the IAF), will have to be retired. Surely its replacement will be quieter and more fuel efficient. Hopefully, it will be as durable and as effective

Overleaf The team executes a downward bomb-burst. The team's Tsukits are clearly painted in the standard orange and white IAF training colours. At one time the team used a special paint scheme. Appparently, that was before the Magister update and now economic reasons seem to dictate a uniform trainer paint job ... even for the IAF aerobatic demonstration team aircraft

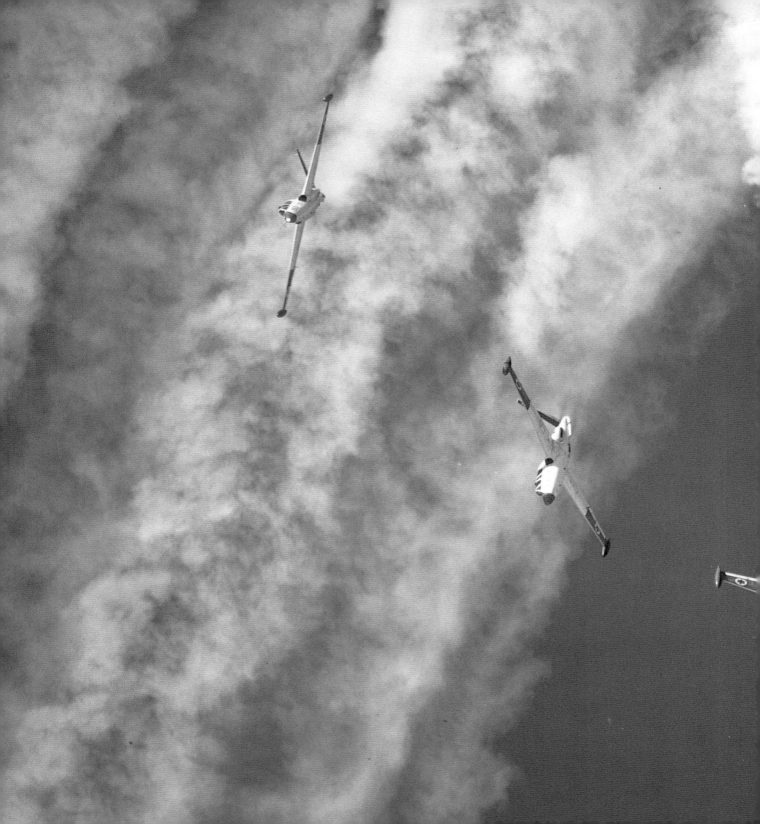

Trailing smoke plumes representing the blue and white colours of Israel, the team executes a pass before an admiring audience of invited guests for the celebration of a class's graduation into the ranks of IAF pilots after a gruelling two year course. Present at the ceremony were the nation's Prime Minister and Defence Minister, as well as the IAF's Commander—Major General Avihu Ben-Nun